You're Already In

HEAVEN

X

10th Anniversary Expanded Edition

Dr. Robin Lloyd Futoran

4th Edition

2020

You're Already In

Heaven

X

HEALING MANKIND PROJECT

www.drrobinlfutoran.com

drrobinlfutoran@gmail.com

Dr. Robin L. Futoran

Illustrations by Diana Levin

Third Edition March 2012
Fourth Edition X November 2020

Expanded, Revised Version X published 11/20

First published @ AuthorHouse 4/30/2010
Published @ IngramSpark 11/11/20

ISBN: 978-1-4490-8168-3 (sb)
ISBN: 978-1-4490-8169-0 (hb)
ISBN: 978-1-4490-8170-6 (eb)
ISBN: 978-17338050-2-5 (sb)
ISBN: 978-1-7338050-3-2 (eb)

Library of Congress Control Number: 2010904904

CONTENTS

"Physical concepts are free creations of the human mind, and are not, however it may seem, uniquely determined by the external world."

Albert Einstein

For Charles and Amanda

With the greatest love and adoration.
I could never be prouder or more inspired.

DIVINE ORDER

As you read these words,

Everything in your life is exactly as it is supposed to be.

Preface

Waking in that state of, "not feeling quite awake," my conscious awareness still suspended in the ecosphere of dreams, afloat in a soup of higher consciousness, of universal consciousness. Feeling connected to every-thing that is or ever was, my thinking mind suspended in the dreamy ethers of oneness while straining under the confines of a pre-frontal cortex whirring quicker than a spinning top, the subconscious mind attempting to restore an earthly sense of order and security. Boundless volumes of inexplicable information beyond known physics surging through my mind while intuition less restrained by material-world limitations remained keenly open to The Energy That Is Everything (TETIE). Sensing the nature of my spiritual self as an infinite being of energy, networking with higher consciousness as it taps into the depths of my physical mind, powerfully attuned to and processing every voice, thought, feeling, emotion, experience and idea that ever was or will be. A lightness of being, a fusion with all physical matter, interconnected to the energetic source of all that is. Symbolic memories and figures linger in infinite space, final bits hovering of many dreams that night. Like a vintage radio receiver, the mind strains to absorb all knowledge and experiences of the universes, teetering between consciousness, unconsciousness, the world of dreams, reality and the waking world. If I could only remember it all. An explosive instant of possessing all knowledge, all love and compassion while simultaneously retaining and knowing nothing. I gracefully slip from the shadow of the non-physical realm into a physical domain.

As quickly as possible I write every thought and feeling, all I can remember in the present moment fused within a lingering dreamscape while striving to avoid the loss of any symbol or message. My mind takes an intentional step up in consciousness, contemplating as an outside observer chronicling the distinction between a dream state, consciousness, unconsciousness, the thinking mind, soul, spirit and the physical domain from the non-physical world. Were my thoughts and feelings originating from random biochemical reactions in my brain or from some higher state of self, from a spiritual realm beyond my body?

Who was in the driver's seat of my thinking? What was initiating any single thought. If ideas were simply the result of physiological biochemistry, what was jump-starting those chemical reactions? I knew I was far more than a handful of minerals and liquids driven indiscriminately by random biochemical reactions in my motionless primitive brain.

Over the following six months, each morning on waking in this altered state of consciousness between worlds, I journaled the awareness and insights swirling these questions. Week after week I found myself differentiating subjects of mind, body, consciousness, physics, metaphysics, thoughts, the brain, neuroanatomy, unconsciousness, the mind, spirit, soul and physical matter. One morning I realized that several weeks had passed without experiencing that altered state or recording dreams and impressions related to those original questions. Upon reviewing the resultant, somewhat readable stack papers on my nightstand, I realized there was information that might be worth sharing.

I avoided telling this part of my story in the first three editions of this book. It was too *woo-woo* and out of character for my clinical practitioner persona. Well, we now know that the proverbial cat is out of the bag. The spiritual, healing cat that is. My work over the last dozen years and practice in healing, functional medicine and health coaching has allowed me to express truths I had been hiding, including this one.

4

My goal in writing this book remains the same. To clarify, make understandable and differentiate how all the preceding concepts fit together. The material is a fusion of resources from those dreams, the altered state between dream and wakefulness, research, life experiences, study in science, spirituality, metaphysics and my understanding from a divinely guided path towards self-realization and intuition. My journey began as a child, has flourished and continues without end. It remains an unending journey, a quest for spiritual truth and a pilgrimage towards perpetual love, peace, harmony and joy.

Infused with the original papers of 2010, this new X publication representing the 10th anniversary of *You're Already in Heaven,* is an expanded version of the original book, clarifying and reframing concepts for a clearer understanding of certain perspectives based on my ongoing transformational evolution and studies in religions, faith, spiritual beliefs, science and theologies of all types. Combining this knowledge and experience with critical reasoning, meditation, expanded consciousness and deep self-introspection, I have come to conclusions of acceptance or rejection of spiritual and scientific concepts based on inner truth for myself.

This book is not about religion, but rather a guide to understanding the eternal spiritual nature of who we are and how living each purely divine and adventurous moment of life generates meaning, purpose and manifests our dreams.

My intention is to humbly present an easy, comfortable understanding for seekers of inner truth, peace and spiritual knowledge whatever their chosen path, broadening each reader's understanding of consciousness, unconsciousness, physical and non-physical matter and spirituality. I trust that all those seeking higher consciousness or greater spirituality will find benefit within these pages bringing them greater love, happiness and life contentment.

Though I make no claim for being the ultimate source of knowing or understanding consciousness, metaphysics, God or spirituality, for me, this is absolute truth and correct. Some concepts, thoughts and communication related to spirituality and God are truly incommunicable with words as we know them. I've done my best to offer in simple terms, a refreshing and expansive perspective on these subjects.

I am hoping to reawaken or reveal to those who are open and interested, that place of infinite love, peace, harmony and joy which are always present and available in each moment of our lives.

We have everything we need to be happy,

Always.

Rejoice!

HEAVEN IS AT HAND.

Heaven Is Not A Goal.

Heaven Is Not a Place

Disengage from the Illusion that Physical Matter is as it Appears.
Physical Matter is Not Solid as you may have *Believed*.

Experience Infinite Harmony in the Perfection of this very Divine Moment!

All it takes is a little practice,

Immersing yourself within
that Eternal Divine Energy that is Everything.

Bathing generously in the bright white light of
each present and vibrant moment.

Be grateful, for you already have all that is necessary

To Live Your Life in Heaven.

The following pages are a guided journey into your

Eternal Nature.

This path weaves its way through dream states, through the
soul, the mind, from consciousness, thoughts and feelings, to
subconsciousness, meditative states and to that which lies
beyond death.

Most importantly, this can be a transformational adventure
Leading us back to our Divinely Spiritual Selves,
Back to that every present place where we are living life in
Heaven.

Prepare to be Empowered.

Defining and understanding the idea of words such as, *consciousness, thoughts, soul, mind* and how they relate to both our physical and spiritual selves is far more complex than a few simple lines authored across a page.

To more easily and thoroughly grasp these concepts, our journey begins with something more familiar.

Dreams.

Chapter I

DREAMS AND
OUR GREATER SPIRITUAL SELF

In the twilight of drifting off to sleep, consciousness heightens, the physical world fading away, our spiritual presence, the being of *energy* we truly are frees and expands beyond the physical realm, reconnecting once again, with our true nature, far from the adhesive binding us to material restraints and barriers of the mind and physical world.

In a luminous instant impossible for confining the greater energy of our true selves, higher consciousness and our spiritual nature, burst courageously and diffusely into the multifaceted fabric of the universe.

While some may eat or drug themselves into oblivion or over-work their minds and body to exhaustion in avoidance and fear of dreaming or permitting any awareness of dreams,

No matter how hard we try, uncontrollably, we drift into largely indescribable, extraordinary and expansive adventures where Dreams will be taking place whether we choose to remember any part of them or not, every night.

When we dream, we are anything but asleep,

And far from *unconscious*.

What if I told you that when Dreaming

You are in the real world,

And when awake,

You are living an illusion?

A dream-state is that same place we travel during meditation, where we more easily manifest and formalize our current existence.

From our dreams, intentions and desires

Create our physical reality.

When we sleep, our body is resting and rejuvenating while Higher Consciousness is connecting to our Greater Spiritual Selves,

That energy of who we really are,

In a higher state of awareness unrestrained by time, space or physical matter,

> We are creating, learning, studying, listening, manifesting, playing, healing and communicating,

As an enormously vibrant, exceedingly omnipresent and active Being of Energy.

Any given night, within even a single dream of many, our greater selves of energy cover vaster distances of time and space and accomplish more than is possible in an entire earthly lifetime.

Free of our physical body and attachments to the material world,

We are more purely connected to our Divinity,
To our authentic Self.

       We are more undividedly integrated within the oneness of

       The Energy That is Everything.

With our body at rest in sleep;

We see, know and behave more purely as

The eternal Spiritual Beings we are,

Operating within many parallel realities, innumerable planes of consciousness and throughout a multitude of universes.

It is from our dreams,

We uniquely create and embrace an indescribable volume of activity without limitations of time or space.

We are returned to our Eternal State.

During wakeful hours,

With significant limitations of human language and comprehension, the only words coming close to describing these multiple planes of reality might include a combination of, past, present, future, parallel electromagnetic fields, the multiverse, String Theory, heaven, universal consciousness, the biofield, celestial energy, love, divine energy, The Energy That Is Everything and I Am.

Within this multitude of parallel realities and planes of existence, time and space are not as we understand them in this physical world.

They don't exist.

Modes of communication, understanding and interpretation of information, projection or manifestation of creative realization are immensely incomparable to what and how we learn throughout earthly incarnations.

Though most of us have little conscious awareness throughout a waking day,

Our brains and minds through the conduit of consciousness are continuously bombarded by bits of information from all these multiple planes of spiritually energetic and universal reality.

We are just too distracted by activities of the day to notice.

Unfortunately, the human brain and nervous systems are too primitive to consciously absorb, learn, interpret and understand all available information. Besides, our minds are overwhelmed and distracted by the waking world of our current incarnation combined in addition to anatomical and physiological limitations.

> While we are of a superior order compared to other living creatures on earth, it is anatomically and physiologically impossible to process and understand immensity and complexity of our world beyond the physical. We do have *some* understanding.

Science confirms that through the human biofield, everyone on the planet is energetically connected not only to one another but also to the earth.

Current consensus is that while energy is transmitted and received by every cell of the body, the primary connection is made through electromagnetic energy emitted from the heart then mind.

One Great Heart.

The Energy That Is Everything.

Throughout a dream state, we are:

Interacting and communicating with anyone we choose, past, present and in the future,

We are more clearly connected to the place of our origin,

Beings of energy flowing with grace and ease within the great ocean of energy that is all of us. The energy that is every living thing.

We move freely and spontaneously throughout the vast universes of love within The Energy That Is Everything.

When sleeping and dreaming without the distractions of wakefulness,

Our true nature as beings of pure energy is manifesting our physical reality, creating physical matter within this plane of existence and many others.

We are connected to the energy of our origin.

We are the energy of our origin,

The same energy of everything that lives.

We are a unique extension of:

The Energy That Is Everything

We Are everything.

Melting into the slumbering domains of sleep and dreams,
Always present, Consciousness does not detach from our waking selves,

Rather we stop paying attention to our current physical state.
We escape all distraction from this worldly incarnation.

Our Spiritual Selves loosen from the confines of the physical world, rising out of and beyond our conscious and unconscious mind, fluidly permeating the ethers for an easy transition into expansive multitudes of parallel realities.

> Modern Quantum Physics has come to terms with multiple parallel planes of reality, realizing there must be at least ten or eleven dimensions for validation of the current *Theory of Everything*; both the M Theory and String Theory.
> All indications though, point to the probability of infinitely more planes of existence.

While our Spiritual-Self functions at very high levels connected to these multiple planes of reality in every moment, even during waking hours, we can have far greater awareness, are far more connected, dynamically active and more genuinely within our true nature when our physical bodies are at total rest.

From the abundance of innumerable planes of existence within the wealth and diversity connected to higher consciousness, beyond time and space, our spiritual selves thrive, yielding unique, spontaneous, creative activities, experiences and actions resulting in revolutionary ideas throughout this incarnation.

By opening our hearts and minds to these heavenly worlds of wonder, through mindful practices, we can tap into this timeless world of everything that exists and ever has or will, from our eternal position within *The Energy That is Everything* during waking hours as well as in a dream state.

Dreams are passages, permitting our spiritual self to function more prominently from our place of origin, from our connection to The Energy That Is Everything, while still having a human experience.

You might think of being in a dream state, as having transitioned from our present inherent human incarnation with all its learned and limiting concepts of self and reality, back into our divinity.

The capacity to be present within this divine region of multiverses during wakeful hours is suppressed by human nature in its patterns of distraction, limitations in thinking, self-absorption and a lack of the anatomical ability for deciphering and understanding the immensity of our nature as spiritual beings of energy.

With a freer and deeper connection to the Divine Source of Everything in dreams or wakefulness;

We can more easily realize our intentions, projections and plans for creating and inspiring the actions for manifesting whatever we desire in this physical incarnation.

We (in our true nature as Spiritual Beings of energy) live and work in a more focused and powerful way during dreams while the distraction of our human-ness and layers of learned information and behaviors solidified over time to this physical plane are placed aside during earthly rest.

> A dream-state acting as the conduit for our higher functioning Spiritual Self reveals an opportunity for intensified actions in a multitude of realities, giving multi-tasking an entirely new meaning.

But there is a problem in reaping the full benefits of a dream state. The amount of information, the Language(s) and understanding of concepts from other time/space realities being accessed during dreams are mostly beyond our human capacity to understand and too overwhelming to attempt.

On waking in the morning if we choose to remember a dream, we must have something humanly understandable to remember. Our neuroanatomy might otherwise be overloaded with information that we cannot possibly interpret leading to feelings of distress.

Instead, our Spiritual Self feeds the human brain bits of images, symbols and ideas that could be interpreted in a more comfortable and understandable ways. Accurate or not, our brain will always fabricate safe and secure interpretations for every situation.

> And that is only if we are willing to have any awareness of information received from dreams in the first place.

Many people choose to avoid knowing what they may have experienced, where they had been or what might have learned and accomplished during a particular dream state.

At the initial moment of waking from sleep, we remain most attuned to our spiritual and more deeply conscious selves. We flow freely between dream state, our spiritual self, the mind, consciousness, thought, subconsciousness and the multiple planes of existence.

> On waking, knowledge of activities that just took place in this recent state of physical rest, adventures we may have enjoyed, experiences of our spiritual selves and action taken, are all still close to the mindful surface.

Almost immediately though, in an initial attempt to remember the vast occurrences taking place during dreams,

> Our humanness, neuro-anatomy and life experience throughout this incarnation begin placing the limited perspectives and barriers to the understanding of metaphysical and highly spiritual spaces, activities and events we just ventured from.

On waking from sleep, our connection to the Divine Energy;

> That location of one's originality, intuitiveness, spontaneity, creativity, empowerment and spirituality,

Can so easily be sidetracked and thrust sharply into the background of our mind out of fear or inattention as we are suddenly and so overwhelmingly re-focused on this physical world, filled with learned, limited concepts for what is possible and more even more, what is impossible.

Information, activities and experiences from our exceptionally energized dream states are so profoundly diffused within multiple realities and contain vast amounts of humanly inexplicable information, it is impossible for our current neuro-anatomy and physiology to translate it into an understandable language.

Besides, most people not ready or unwilling to understand even what they think they might like to know from a dream.

Our spiritual selves understand that human nature, learned behaviors, thoughts and human neuroanatomy have significant limitations in understanding the vast subjects of non-matter or metaphysical subjects and experiences.

To feel comfortable and feel safe about dream experiences, our spiritual self through consciousness as a conduit to thoughts in our mind, pares down the plethora of information to the smallest bit of what was experienced and manifested. This leads to the framing of simple, understandable perspectives by means of symbols and visual stories allowing only information we are prepared to know or understand in that moment.

When we have no recollection or understanding of our dream, which is common, we are just not yet ready to know the truth of what was revealed during that particular dream space.

Remembering a dream is a choice.

Having immortal strength, knowing our eternal presence, healing the sick, healing ourselves, soaring like an eagle, transforming ourselves, shape-shifting, helping others and the planet, being someone else, saving the world in some fashion and reaching heights that seem otherwise impossible might all be the most miniscule portion of a typical dream adventure.

> At a first wakeful thought, majestic, powerful feelings still lingering, physical awareness and mental reflection on the dream bring immediate dimming of memories, the grand feeling wane while placing earthly, understandable thoughts and feelings based on learned beliefs and neuroanatomical limitations in our ability to process the information.

High effort arm flapping only to stay inches above the ground may replace the grandeur of soaring like an eagle or flying through space.

The chronicles of human experience combined with learned, limiting thoughts and memories need understandable concepts to grasp. Since it is learned that humans are unable to fly, the dream interpretation is that of silly arm flapping while sinking back to earth.

> Being *unable* to fly is far more believable for us as humans even though far grander accomplishments and feats will have been accomplished during dreams.

As our consciousness expands to include the limitless nature of our spiritual selves, we might instead begin to live from that place of higher probability allowing soaring as eagles, healing humankind and saving the planet to be valid and possible.

Our *willingness-to-understand the results of dream work* will be the only limitation as to what is remembered or understood in the morning.

We could choose to have the complete answer,

To discover only a small insightful bit of information open to interpretation,

Or we might choose to remember nothing at all.

The choice is ours.

Parts of dreams may be understandable and directly linked to our current physical reality and plane of existence.

Simultaneously within other areas of the same dream space, our spiritual self is undertaking an abundance of tasks and pursuing other quests in a myriad of diverse realities.

These many planes of existence are indefinable by human language, interpretation, logic, words and physical properties as we know them.

This is one reason dreams are so easily misunderstood to be an involuntary, random series of images, thoughts, emotions, fantasies and visions.

There is nothing further from truth.

Intentional, purposeful and productive work can be accomplished during each night's dream state.

It is Powerful.

It is Spectacular.

Dreams in the same manner as meditation, might be considered

Powerful, vibrant Spiritual Field Trips,

Beyond our physical constraints and self-imposed limitations.

During our Dreams,

Guidance can be discovered on any subject in one's life.

The perfect steps to an objective or goal revealed.

Any question answered.

New paths and ideas uncovered.

Healing and improvement of health for yourself and others.

Truths divulged.

All you have to do is be willing and open to your personal truth.

Pre-sleep affirmations are one method for guiding our Spiritual Intentions in,

Acquiring knowledge, generating positive life actions, healing ourselves and others, answering important questions, having guidance in life's next steps, manifesting physical reality and sparking energetic thoughts that stimulate, transform and generate physical matter.

Simple pre-sleep *Dream Generating* affirmation

"Tonight, I'm going to dream.

The dream will be big, clear and in color.

I will gain guidance:

...in direction for ...,

...for an answer to ...,

...to resolve and understand the problem in my relationship /
work,

(or whatever the life question might be).

The answer will be clear,
and I will remember it in the morning."

**

Whether seeking guidance for health, career, love, prosperity, a physical achievement, an educational direction or a quest related to any life issue,

Be specific in your affirmation about what you want to know or see.

Writing the question or intention in a Dream Journal will strengthen your ability to remember.

Repeat the affirmation until you feel sure beyond words and thoughts that, without a doubt, you will have the dream and you will remember it. Repeat the affirmation in your mind or aloud until you feel it to be true within every cell of your body.

> Know deep in the fiber of your being, that when you wake in the morning, you will remember the dream and have the answer you were looking for.

> An answer will always show itself if you really want to know.

Practicing intentional dream work nightly can bring and a new world of knowledge, information, guidance and manifestation.

To further enhance the clarity and power of your dream work, keep a journal or pad and pen next to the bed. Before sleep, write the question or guidance you are seeking in this journal,

When you wake in the morning or during the night, write down anything you can remember of your dream. Even if it is only one word or thought. Often, once you begin recording your dream, greater detail will unfold a whole new world of information and memories from multiple dreams.

Interpreting dreams is an art, not a science.

Avoid being attached to meanings for images, symbols, stories and people that are familiar.

While having the answer you seek, Dream symbols may seem completely unrelated to your intended dream work.

With numerous possibilities,

There is always only *one* accurate dream interpretation that

Feels Personally True

No matter what symbols, people and stories are remembered.

Only you know that truth.

Feelings (intuition) during dreams are more powerful and
significant interpreters than what was seen or heard.

Say for instance you fall asleep with the intention to dream of an abundance of money coming to you from an unexpected place. On waking, the dream you remember is that of being chased into a cave by a frightening animal where you surprisingly find family or friends you try to warn of this pending doom though they appear un-phased. You wake feeling anxious and frightened.

This small bit of what really transpired during a much larger dream experience could seem unrelated to the intended work. But notice the feelings of the situation. The fear may have been related to not having needed money and the animal representing mounting bills. Family and friends not being afraid for you or themselves might indicate that the fear is unwarranted. It may be that family and friends are the source of unexpected funds coming available or guidance. There may have been a lesson in the wealth of family and friends being greater than money.

Ultimately the result of that dream work may be that money or abundance is manifested in ways you still have not imagined.

This example when not considering more details from the dream, time of day, color, black and white, weather, ages of yourself and those around you, feelings about each symbol and person, makes the experience uni-planar and far simpler than the multi-dimensional nature of a dream and all the possibilities for interpretation. There are many resources to assist you in dream interpretation.

Most important is not to get stuck trying to understand dream symbols in their literal sense.

There will always be several possible interpretations, but only one that

Feels Right

And *fits* your specific dream intention.

The rational mind will work towards quick interpretations allowing you to feel emotionally safe while obscuring information that you might be apprehensive to learn.

Historical records reveal Abraham Lincoln frequently shared dreams with certain members of his cabinet. They recount his regularly gaining guidance and making important decisions during the civil war based on information gleaned in his dreams.

During the weeks prior to his assassination, Lincoln was reported to have dreamt of seeing himself being mourned at his own funeral.

The Physical – Consciousness – and The Source

In dreams or wakefulness,

An undisrupted relationship is maintained between our mind, consciousness, spiritual self -

And divine source of our origin.

Our true nature as beings of Spiritual Energy remains an eternal extension of and from within that source.

This perpetual union provides the foundation for manifesting our physical reality.

When every action and thought is flowing naturally and authentically from the place of our origin,

We can perform what might be considered

Miracles.

Endless physical world distractions diverge awareness of that perpetual connection to our Spiritual Self.

Incessant diversions of the body and mind might include visual and auditory stimulation, hoarding, computer activities, zombie scanning cell phones, gaming, electronic device use, drugs, shopping, obsessive hobbies, gambling, reading, studying, eating, alcohol, sleeping, movies, binge watching tv shows, physical and emotional neediness, exercise, medication, sex, love and other addictions.

This over stimulation,

Personal obsessive behaviors,

> Are effusive, sometimes unnoticed deterrents to the awareness of the continuous and distinct connection to our authentic nature, to the Divinely Spiritual Beings we truly are.

These actions and distractions contribute to a mental and emotional laziness, reducing our ability to reason, think logically and expand our neuro-anatomical and physiological capacities,

Resulting in a sluggishness of our neuro-anatomical ability to creatively process information associated with our multi-dimensional Spiritual Self.

Over time, weakness develops in connecting to higher states of consciousness,

Reducing interest in taking bold actions in life and manifesting our greatest dreams and desires.

In other words, physical-world distractions separate us from our authentic, spiritual selves, disempowering our interest in the pursuit of powerful meaning, purpose and big life adventures.

In effect, our physical ability, mental aptitudes and aspirations become complacent.

The energy of who we are becomes contracted and constricted more firmly rooted within the world of solid matter and confines of physical laws.

We forgot the magic of who we truly are and skills we possess,

Creating and maintaining fixed patterns of who *we think we are* and what we *believe* possible or impossible based on learned limitations and narrow perceptions by what we have experienced in physical form.

Think of, *walking through life wearing blinders* to greater possibility.

Ultimately, our connection to *The Energy That is Everything*, the energy of our origin, of our authentic self, is pushed further into the background and radically diminished.

Completely tuning-out your connection to Divine Source as you move through daily activities and life, is *a Choice*.

Detachment from awareness of one's Spiritual Self,

From the connection to The Energy That Is Everything,

May be a life-long trek as in,

Living Unconsciously.

Negative, thoughts, actions and distractions are artificial barriers to behaving from or reaching, higher states of spiritual awareness or connecting to our higher consciousness.

Acting in unconscious ways by participating or focusing on artificial physical stumbling blocks,

We miss opportunities to create, manifest and prosper from a place of higher consciousness.

We miss out on valuable experiences, growth and transformation!

Ideally, we overcome the self-devised physical barriers and distractions to higher consciousness that create self-mistrust in hearing, knowing and taking actions from our purest place of intention and truth.

The closer we are to wisdom revealed through our bond with *The Energy That Is Everything*, the more our thoughts and actions in physical time and space express our truth.

Acting from a place of authenticity arising from our spiritual truth,

We flourish in abundance, love, peace and joy.

The good news: *It's A Choice.*

You can live your life with greater connection to your authentic nature.

You can live your life with more Meaning, Purpose and Joy,

You can live a more Empowered Life.

You can live In Full Participation.

Make the decision *Now*.

Choose to live big with Meaning, Purpose and Joy.

Allow and cultivate awareness of your special connection to
The Energy That Is Everything, your origin and home.

Live from within the flow of Divine Knowledge

United with your supernatural-ness.

Let dreams and meditation be effortless spaces for connecting to that divine origin,

Where you plan, create and compose your physical world.

Perfectly blended with The Energy That Is Everything,

We act from our authentic place of expansive, creative, spontaneous, love, peace, harmony and joy, manifesting opportunities for every best and appropriate life choice and action.

We are the Divine Energy that is everything,

Even when we are not in a dream state.

When we are connected to the Eternal Energy that is
Everything, the Divine Source of our Origin,

Heaven is at Hand.

What is *Divine Source?*

In the simplest of terms as a concept beyond words and human explanation, communication or language,

Divine Source
(god as you know and understand her)

Omnipotent, Omniscient, Omnipresent,

Is that place of Oneness with Everything.

A place of the greatest love and highest truth.

Divine Source is where we are all connected

The origin of Every-Thing.

The most comprehensive words I find to describe the Divine Source of everything, is:

The Energy That Is Everything

(TETIE)

It is the nature of existence.

Whether we realize or accept that connection,

We do not live without being connected to TETIE.

TETIE does not exist without being connected to us.

We are one in the same.

There is no choice.

Every-Thing

Is a manifestation of Energy,

Of The Energy That Is Everything.

To better understand this concept, let us look to science and the study of:

The Theory of Everything.

An ongoing search by modern day physicists, The Theory of Everything began thousands of years ago. It is *the search for the smallest particle in the universe.*

Physicists believe that this smallest particle will prove to be the origin of all physical matter providing a commonly used reference for studying The Theory of Everything as:

The search for the:

God Particle

A glimpse into the *Atom* will help us understand the energetic nature of all physical matter.

Atomism first described by Leuccippus in the 5th century B.C.E. was based on a theory that every living object in nature was composed of space (void) and atoms. These atoms were thought to be the smallest indivisible fraction of matter and in constant motion. After nearly 2,500 years (into the late 19th century) of scientists referring to these particles, there was finally evidence that these atoms existed. But, it was then discovered that these atoms were not the smallest elements in nature and could be further broken down into even smaller bits of physical matter known as protons, neutrons and electrons.

In the last century it was found that protons, neutrons and electrons making up atoms could be broken down into smaller units identified as quarks, gluons, leptons and hadrons.

Later, these bits of matter were further identified to be consisting of vibrating strings (The String Theory).

In the latest model, the M Theory, three or four of the String Theories are combined to explain the *God Particle*.

Okay, are you getting the picture?

All these theories are masterful, science-minded, logical, hypothetical guesses that may not be physically proven for thousands of years if ever.

Next, if strings are proven it will be discovered that strings are made of something else even smaller.

The search will be endless.

After several more millennia of searching and reducing particles to smaller and smaller components,

Scientists will reach a point where the tinniest particles are finally broken down to nothing.

No-Thing.

The penultimate, most infinitesimal bit of physical matter disappears.

Becomes No Physical Matter.

The ultimate discovery in physical science will be that the smallest particle in nature

Is simply a physical manifestation

Of energy.

The search can be halted!

"The Theory of Everything"

is simple.

It is

Energy

The God Particle is

ENERGY.

The Energy That Is Everything

The God Particle is

Energy

Vibrating in specific patterns and varying densities creating unique and different types of physical matter.

No matter how dense or hard the physical nature of an object,

It is still composed of Energy.

Everything in nature is composed of Energy in its purest most dynamic form.

There is one Existence:

One Being,

Tremendous, Limitless, Infinite and Immeasurable.

One Consciousness and One Energy.

This One Divine Spiritual Energy,

The source of all things,

The Energy That Is Everything,

Is being expressed in Quadrillions and Quadrillions
of unique Life Forms.

With infinite incarnations and variations in choices of form, density and structure,

> All living organisms, each with their unique physical components and appearing as solid matter,

> Are simply unique expressions of and from within

> *The Energy That Is Everything.*

The Energy That is Everything, Universal Consciousness,
God by any name,

Does Not Discriminate.

In the eyes of the one Energy That Is Everything,

No one thing, person or creature,

Is better, more deserving

Or in greater favor than anyone else,

No matter how hard a person tries to be special in the eyes of God,

Whether a religious leader, through prayer and meditation, reading, studying or devotion,

All Living Creatures, All Living Things,

Are Equal in the eyes of God,

As is true for the earth, the sun and the rain serving every living creature equally,

The Energy of our Origin,

Is impartial to all.

Love, Compassion, Healing and Support are present equally for everyone.

God does not judge or punish,

Only man judges and punishes,
including himself.

God judges no more than an apple tree chooses who is
worthy of picking its apples.

No matter how you think, what you say or do,

It is Impossible to be Un-Loved by God.

As the sun shines no brighter on a Saint,

All Are Equal in the Eyes of God.

If a Thought or Behavior Divides Us,

It is Not of God.

If it Unites Us,

It is of God.

The Dao says;

Rather than judge,

Love, Respect and Cherish.

Have Awareness, Experience and Love.

Inexhaustibly Infused by

The Energy That Is Everything,

We Humans have an Infinite Capacity for
Experiencing and Sharing Love,
Compassion and Healing

The more we use, the more there is.

We each have the ability to experience, a rapturous, life-altering, transcendent, god-uniting spiritual encounter

with

The Energy That Is Everything,

Just as the most powerful religious and spiritual leaders throughout history.

Connecting with God,

Having a transcendent experience with the energy of our origin,

Is not something achieved through reading books, in lessons from teachers and is not found in words, names or buildings.

Heavenly, God-Uniting, Transformative Bliss

Is an Experience.

A Spiritual Experience

Does not have to involve religion, belief or faith.

A Spiritual Experience

Can Be one of

A Deep Sense of Meaning and Purpose,

A Deep Connection to Universal Truth,

A Deep Sense of Love

Spirituality = Love

Love = The Energy That Is Everything (TETIE)

TETIE = God by any name.

Tools might be employed for reaching a spiritual connection, for opening the doors of perception and awareness to The Energy That Is Everything,

Including methods, such as, meditation, prayer, chanting, dancing, breathing, affirmations, communing with nature and singing to name just a few.

While any method or practice in itself holds no spiritual answer or truth, they function as a medium, a stepping stone for getting the human brain and physical-self out of the way, opening the heart and mind to the always present energy of our origin.

A Blissful, Spiritual Experience is always available.

We Know when it happens.

We Know when a true Spiritual Connection takes place.

There is no need to explain or justify being embodied by
the Love or seeing through the eyes of God.

We opened the spiritual door to direct contact with
universal consciousness,

The experience is precisely and entirely for us,

Between Us and our Maker.

No description could ever come close to explaining a Spiritual Experience,

> That profoundly divine experience of merging in the oneness of Love, of God's love, within universal consciousness, uniting with The Energy That Is Everything.

Besides, an individual's reality and experience are unique. It is a manufactured, individual illusion developed over time and through life experience designed to create familiarity, habit and survival.

> We can never truly know someone else's experience.

That said, descriptions of Spiritual Experiences have included terms and ideas, such as,

Vibrant sensations within every cell and atom of the body, explosive, endlessly expansive, a liberation from everything physical, detachment from all thoughts and feelings, a magnificent sense of lightness and space, a oneness with all that exists, an explosive, vibrant infusion within the one great energy, empowering strength and courage, love and peace, compassion, power, a floating within the vibrant pool of pure love and godliness, ecstatic love, soaring within the heavens, untethered freedom, a knowing of all that is, seeing through the eyes of universal consciousness / God, a most ecstatic indescribable feeling of Love for no reason.

Universal Oneness Becomes Your State.

Eternal Divine Bliss,

Is Ever Present.

Every physical organism on this planet individually and in combination, everything beyond physics (metaphysical), outside the known universes and all their components including each vibrating atomic and subatomic particle,

Embody the matrix of

The Energy That Is Everything

With lack of world consensus for any single word, description, definition, belief or intention for a Spiritual Source.

God, Allah, Buddha, Elohim, Brahman, Shang Ti, Kwannon, Abraxas, Sat-chit-ananda, Tasawwuf, Bhagavan, Jehovah, OM or by any other name, all have the same intended meaning and purpose.

All are rooted in the same place,

They are the same entity,

They are all of and within:

The Energy That Is Everything

Every physical and non-physical structure having arisen out of unique vibrant arrangements of energy, from quantum subatomic particles to the macroscopic planets, cosmos and beyond, the energy of individual and collective consciousness, thoughts and subconsciousness in total,

Are God by any name.

Divine, Omnipresent, Omniscient, Omnipotent

are

The Energy That Is Every-Thing.

In our multi-planar existence, united as one within collective consciousness and everything that is or ever has been, more easily attuned through dream states and meditation (or after death),

> We have the potential for accessing divine resources in creating physical matter and generating big life opportunities, far beyond the typical limitations of our human mind, thoughts and beliefs.

Mindful practices, such as, meditation, prayer, Qigong, journaling, communing with nature and positive affirmations aide in removing mental and physical barriers preventing our body and mind from being more closely connected to our Spiritual Source, to:

The Energy That Is Everything

Tapping into your Intuition, *sense, feel and know* that which exists beyond your learned and observable world,

Allow natures connection with everything that is,

With The Energy That Is Everything.

Simply be open to the probability that your eternal nature as Spiritual Energy, your *soul*, extends well beyond the limitations of your physical body.

> How often have you sat or laid on a surface, realizing you could not sense where your body ended and the surface began.
> Or holding the hand of another person when you realize that you are unable to define where your skin ends and theirs begins.

Our Spiritual Self,

The energy of who we truly are,

Is vastly greater and more expansive than anything our brain and minds can contain or comprehend, and far more extensive than the limitations of our physical body.

Historically referenced by some of the greatest philosophers, spiritual and psychosocial leaders and now by quantum physicists,

We are Spiritual Beings having a

Human Experience.

Every living thing, including human beings, are a unique
extension of and from within,

The Energy That is Everything

"Faith is taking the first step, even when you don't see the whole staircase."

Martin Luther King.

Chapter II

CONSCIOUSNESS, SUBCONSCIOUSNESS, SOUL AND SPIRITUALITY

Human beings may have the capacity for more complex, creative thinking, logic and verbal expression when compared to most life-forms.

We humans also have greater physical agility and aptitude compared to most other living things. These characteristics result from our unique neuroanatomy and physiology

But,

Every living thing equally embodies a soul, a Spiritual Self and Consciousness.

Really?

Who Are You?

Are you your name?

Tina, Amanda, Charles, Heather, Max, Chanda, Bennett, Lavar, Renee, Nash, Matt, Caroline, Gerry, Dale, Linda, Diana, Barry, Patsy, Rose, Sandi, Steffi, Jamal, Lisa, Eka, Tammy, Kylee, Kim, Jaqueline, Ed, Jesse, Trenton, Davette, Hadi, Larry, Troy, Kristy, Reese...

Did you come into this world with a name attached to you?

Are you the words or letters contained in your name?

Of course not.

Someone made up a name for you. Maybe justifying it with earthly meaning, but grabbed it out of the sky.

Very helpful for social and human interaction, you were tagged with this *label*, using agreed upon symbols (letters), representing a fabricated language, making it easier to identify you and for others to catch your attention without saying, *hey you*.

There are others who have your same name/label even though they are not you.

A name is a contrived a label identifying your physical self during this incarnation. It is a symbol, aiding other in identifying you as a unique physical being.

You are not your name.

Are you, how you describe yourself?

A Mother, Father, teacher, lawyer, hairdresser, doctor, son, daughter, CEO, cashier, cook, friendly, truck driver, nurse, loving, mean, giving, strong, frail, kind, open, caring, adventurous, arrogant, extrovert, introvert, self-centered, curious, will power, intelligent, optimistic, competent, silly, fun, energetic, fearful, pessimistic...

No.

We build an illusion of a world within the *confines of our mind*, creating a *package* of specific thoughts, feelings, emotions and behaviors for *who we think we are* for projecting to the outside world. A conceptual model of self.

But these are only social roles and ways you imagine yourself to be, partly shaping behaviors. They are informational footprints of the past and present, personality traits. We retain labels and experiences attempting to orientate ourselves within a culture and family while also protecting ourselves and drawing distinctions relative to other humans. They are bids for creating unique characteristics or separateness between who we think we are and other people.

Social roles and personality traits might be compared to wearing clothing.

> Clothes can make a statement.
> You can dress up, look fancy, appear casual and have style,
> Maybe expose yourself as a statement or hide parts you do not want others to see.
> Clothes might act as protection.

The word *Personality* originates from the Latin,

persona,

Meaning Mask.

In other words, personalities, social roles and labels are masks camouflaging our true selves.

You are not a collection of made-up or conditioned roles, past experiences or behaviors.

You are not what you have done or how you have been in your past.

You are Much More.

Are you a Brain and Body?

Carbon, Hydrogen, Oxygen and Nitrogen.

These four elements make up 97% of our physical body. Calcium and Phosphorus added equals over 99% of our physical composition.

The human body is little more than a handful of minerals bloated with liquids, held together by electromagnetic forces and operating on an involuntary adventure of biochemical reactions.

This handful of minerals and liquid moved by powerful metaphysical forces beyond the knowledge and comprehension of modern science,

> Organizes itself into a machine composed of trillions of subatomic particles creating a physical form that includes a powerplant for energy, the ability for movement by bones, muscles and joints, eyes for seeing, ears for hearing, a brain for thinking and together imparting the skills for self-expression.

But that is not who you are.

Our body operates on automatic-pilot, in the same manner as a robot requiring software and an operating system,

Or like a musical instrument, a trumpet, sitting dormant waiting for an outside force to breathe life through its body and hands to support and drive the keys.

Who is breathing life into our physical instrument?

Who is operating our human software?

What is the driving force of a human body?

Where is the source of inspiration and motivation for functioning,

The trigger for each thought, behavior and action?

What is location of the software and operating system?

As Spiritual Beings having a human experience,

The Soul,

Our greater self as

Unique expressions of The Energy That Is Everything,

Is what

Infuses the Life Breath,

The Meaning, Purpose and Desire,

Driving and managing a physical body and human experience.

You are not a handful of minerals,
electromagnetic energy and fluids.

Are you the Thoughts and Voices in your Mind?

That constant barrage of voices in your head analyzing, logical or illogical ideas, debating decisions, describing feelings, emotion and detail of what they experience, gossiping, judging, contemplating, positive voices, negative thoughts, telling you how to think or feel. Who are those voices and who is the listener?

What should I do with..., I will never..., I'm going to..., How many times must..., Why am I not..., When will..., Should I..., Why are they..., Will I ever..., I don't like..., Why did he..., I thought you wanted..., When will she..., Why aren't you..., joyful, depressed, angry, content, happy, fuming, lonely, bored, sad, thirsty, hot, delighted, cold, hungry, love, dislike, lucky, sleepy, resent, ecstatic, energized, mad, successful, hate, tired, positive...

It is an Endless stream of distracting prattle.
Is that who you are?

No.

Narrow, learned, habitual thought patterns and perspectives manifested and stored throughout life, limited by previous, imperfect teachers and experiences, are not who you are.

You are not your problems or successes,

Not the pain, the emptiness, loneliness or joy you might feel.

Those are just thoughts and feelings in your mind.

The Real You,

Is just *Observing.*

You

are the

Witness.

Recognizing yourself as the Observer and not as your thoughts or feelings presents an opportunity for releasing them.

As the Witness of thoughts, feelings and experiences that do not serve you,
        Notice that *they are not you.*

Observe and release negative, stressful emotions and feelings just as you witness leaves drifting by in a stream.

        You are not the thoughts and feelings of your mind.

        You are the Witness.

You *are* the *Listener* and *Observer* of all the chatter.

You are the *Witness* of all that takes place in and outside your mind.

The Witness and Observer of thoughts, feelings, emotions and experiences.

Without the Witness,

Voices of the mind and thoughts do not exist.

You Are the Witness

Who observes experiences, thoughts, mind, feelings, emotions, physical functions and sensations of a human body and the surrounding material world during this incarnation?

But where are you, the Witness?

What is the origin of, and who directs you the Witness?

The Brain, Consciousness and Soul (Spiritual Self)

A choice and typically requiring practice,

The frequency in *awareness* of our spiritual self and
consciousness varies through the interpretative and
collaborative capabilities of our adept, but limited, human
physical and biochemical mechanism;

The Brain.

Consciousness and soul are unique extensions of

The Energy That Is Everything

Occupying no specific point in time or space.

An individual life-form's consciousness and soul inhabit no precise location within its physical anatomy.

Consciousness and Soul are unique, dynamic forces of energy having awareness,

Observing all thoughts, feelings and the physical body.

Consciousness and Soul are Eternal.

Close your eyes, remember looking at your face in a mirror as child.
You might distinctly remember the specifics of what you were observing, sensations in your body, what you were thinking and feeling about how you looked.
Seeing your face in a mirror today, you again listen to thoughts and feelings about the way you look.

But there is one constant,

One thing that has not changed at all, no matter how many years have passed.

You, The Witness.

Looking in a mirror at a physical self,

Unaffected by time or space, unaffected by thoughts, emotion or physical sensation,

Your Eternal Spiritual Nature and consciousness
Are the same.

Throughout each incarnation,

Whatever physical form you choose to take,

Consciousness and who you are as a Spiritual Being
within and as a unique extension of

The Energy That Is Everything,

Remains constant.

Expression of any life-form's Consciousness and Spiritual Self depends on:

The unique physical capability (anatomy, physiology, physical features) to interpret, understand, physically perform and communicate within its present biological environment.

No matter what form a life takes,

Whether a dog, a redwood tree, a dolphin, a blade of grass, a bacterium, a human or a bear,

Every life-form is an equally connected, unique energetic and Spiritual extension of and from within The Energy That Is Everything.

Each life-form having equal Consciousness.

What appears to be different levels of consciousness, intellect or capabilities are simply variations in that entities physical ability (anatomy) to interpret, express and/or communicate its Spiritual and conscious self.

Every living thing, a blade of grass for example, bears the same consciousness and soul as a human.

For a blade of grass in this incarnation though, physical limitations for mobility, communication, taking actions and self-expression do not compare to that of a human. Communication, physicality, life experience and expectancy are that which is typical for a blade of grass.

Consciousness and soul are the same.

Dolphins, dogs and horses are known to be of high intelligence, yet limitations in science have revealed only minor avenues for understanding or communicating with these animals.

Deficiency in technology's ability to understand these animals does not mean they lack a consciousness and spirit equivalent to all living things, including man. They are only absent of comparative anatomy and physiology to express these qualities to humans.

The inability of man to identify, measure, observe and record communication, consciousness and soul of other species and living organisms does not mean it is absent.

Each life form communicates and expresses itself in their own way within its specific community.

All living things having equal soul and consciousness, it might be more accurate to modify the commonly stated:

We are spiritual beings having a human experience,

To:

We are spiritual beings having an earthly experience.

Unlimited choices are accessible for experiencing in any incarnation. At times we may choose karmic opportunities for growth, to further spiritual awakening, have a lesson in new skills. Other times might simply include new, unique adventures of meaning and purpose.

Some incarnations are chosen for creating and some for contemplating, others to be in service or to be served.

An incarnation has no relevance to time and space. Whether choosing to be a mayfly having a life expectancy of several hours or Bristlecone Pine tree living for 5,000 years.

Knowledge, experience, growth, evolution and adventure are derived from each physical form.

Being human in this lifetime does not mean it will interest us or be the choice for our next one.

Soul and Consciousness are not unique to humans.

In the course of a physical experience, interpretation and understanding of concepts beyond the natural world, beyond known matter (metaphysical concepts) and including of our Spiritual and conscious self, is limited by our biological apparatus.

This limitation results from our anatomy's inability to deeply interpret and understand concepts beyond physical nature.

In addition, the volume of information encompassing our multi-dimensional Spiritual Self expanded across unlimited parallel and non-parallel realities would be far too overwhelming for our primitive anatomy (the brain) to interpret, comprehend and communicate.

An effort to have full knowledge and understanding of our metaphysical self, parallel planes of existence and what we truly carry out in the vastness of our dreams and meditation might be likened to an attempt for pouring all the sands of the earth (representing information) through a tiny funnel, into a perfume bottle (being the human brain) and accomplishing this feat in only a few seconds.

Within physics as we understand them on earth, filling a tiny bottle in this manner within few seconds would be an impossible venture, as is trying to fill our human brain with the volumes of knowledge and information our Spiritual Self experiences.

Consciousness is limited in its ability to translate the full nature of our Spiritual Self to the brain not only through neuro-anatomical confines,

But also resulting from our humanly preconceived, learned, subconscious thoughts, judgements, behaviors, fixed beliefs and the absence of a suitable language for communication.

In other words, no matter how hard we try or how much we study, our understanding of anything, will always be based on the limitations of anatomy, physiology and a unique, learned and manufactured preconceived world view.

As a newborn and young child, still being so near to our Spiritual Origin,

> We were better able to know the greater nature of who we are,

>> Though with undeveloped communication skills and ability to express that knowledge.

> Unfortunately, this inborn awareness was progressively obscured and buried in the process of being raised

> Through learning the rules for surviving and thriving in the physical world.

In essence, we are confined in understanding metaphysical matters by our;

Lack of a suitable language and communication skills,

Learned and fixed subconscious, concepts, thoughts, judgements and behaviors related to functioning in a physical reality.

And, by subconscious fears of not really wanting to know all truths.

Subconscious Mind

The *subconscious mind* acts as a *filter* and *vault* for information coming into the brain, channeled through consciousness from our spiritual self, resulting in thoughts and feelings. Our subconscious mind is where we create and store beliefs, learned behaviors, automatic reactions and narrow, rigid self-concepts.

Ninety percent of the time, we act and behave on auto-pilot from the Old Brain (the Amygdala), with learned, limiting beliefs, thoughts and behaviors stored in the subconscious mind.

Doubt, fear, worry, stress, anger, judgements, addictive behaviors, defensiveness, rage, ego, over-reaction and other out-of-control feelings are stored and acted out from the subconscious mind.

These stockpiled, learned thoughts and feelings can block or limit creativity, expanded thinking and our deeper understanding of more complex information from our higher consciousness and spiritual selves.

With practice, willingness and intention, learned subconscious limiting thoughts and ideas interfering with spontaneous, expansive growth and connection to our Conscious and Spiritual selves, can be over-written.

Consciousness

Anatomic and physiological limitations of the subconscious mind render understanding and expressing metaphysical subjects or expanded perspectives of reality difficult throughout a human experience.

Consciousness is the link between the soul and thinking mind. Between our spiritual self and brain.

Consciousness, directly linked to our spiritual self, carries greater knowledge than our brain is able to comprehend. One of its most important activities for consciousness is in paring down and deciphering information emanating from our spiritual self and multiple dimensions into comfortable, useful and orderly bits of information.

The brain's ability to comprehend greater amounts of our spiritual self and metaphysical subjects requires practice and actions that broaden the connection between our brain, thoughts and higher states of consciousness.

Awareness and *intention* are necessary for raising consciousness and over-riding subconscious (unconscious) fixed ideas and beliefs attempting to slow or prevent such expansion.

It's a choice.

As not all humans venture beyond the conscious borders of our fabricated, limiting illusion of self,

A desire for truth, knowledge and understanding is required.

There is always an option of remaining hostage

To the narrow, learned and fixed beliefs by the subconscious mind negating and blocking more empowering and expansive possibilities.

It's a choice.

Awareness of our conscious or Spiritual self is easier within meditation and dream states where the body is at rest and our minds are most dis-associated with the physical environment and old-brain thinking.

We are released from boundaries blocking greater truths imposed by the confines of our brain and have fewer physical distractions.

We are then more fully immersed within the fabric of

The Energy That Is Everything.

Consciousness is separate from the Soul.

The Spiritual Self being an eternal, unique extension of and from within The Energy That Is Everything, has been referred to by many names including, "I Am," the Soul, Love, Spirit, Yang, Light and Atman.

Consciousness is an *attribute* of one's Spiritual Self.

An instrument of sorts.

Consciousness is a characteristic of all living subjects facilitating communication between physical form and our true nature as beings of spiritual energy.

Consciousness is the conduit between one's Spiritual self and the brain during a physical incarnation and allowing thoughts and physical expression.

You might call it the *Interpreter* between

The physical and Spiritual Worlds.

Consciousness is a bridge between our Spiritual Self

and the physical world.

Consciousness operates in concert between the Spiritual self, the brain, between the mind and thoughts, as a channel for observing, guiding and interpreting our place within the nature of metaphysical reality, within physical nature, in creating our world view and how we express a ourselves.

It is a continuous link between a physical incarnation and

The Energy That Is Everything.

Consciousness is an instrument allowing understanding and communication between our Spiritual and physical selves.

Stated another way, consciousness is a tool used by our Spiritual self to communicate, observe and bring information to the physical self for creativity and expression to the degree allowed by the limitations in comprehension of our anatomy and physiology, and obstacles generated from learned, fixed beliefs filtered through our subconscious mind.

This channel of communication also works in the other direction, allowing the human mind and body to send messages to our Spiritual self.

Consciousness
> Guides information and messages communicated between our Spiritual self for the operation and expression of our human mind and body.

Consciousness functions in this physical plane and a multiple of others simultaneously.

Consciousness related to this plane of existence is specific to this incarnation and this world.

Within other planes of existence, consciousness is specific to those positions within other realities.

Consciousness functioning within other planes of reality will have various forms of communications. Using earthly languages as an example,

Imagine knowing only one language, say, English.

We would live in the language of English. We could never understand Greek without accepting its existence or studying Greek. The Greek language would still be present whether we acknowledged and learned it or not.

In the same manner, if we live *only* in Earthly consciousness, we could hardly understand consciousness of other realities.

Living only in Consciousness as we understand it from earthly languages, thoughts and interpretations,

We could never understand Consciousness of other dimensions without being open to their existence and learning the language.

Living and operating in multiple planes of existence simultaneously, our consciousness and Spiritual-self understand an infinite variety of languages within those different realities.

Due to neuro-anatomical limitations and constrained learned-beliefs, we are unable to know and understand these many planes of existence while living and focusing primarily within this earthly incarnation.

> We can though, create opportunities for tapping into the knowledge and experience within at least portions of other planes of existence and be more consciously multilingual through practices, such as, meditation and dream work.

Intention, practice and willingness are keys to expanding consciousness while maintaining a connection to

The Energy That Is Everything.

If you close your eyes, what do you see?

Most people would say nothing. It is dark, blackness.

At the same time, your busy mind might be talking, saying, your body is present, you are sitting on something and somewhere in time and space, there are sounds around you, but you can't see any of the surrounding physical objects.

You the Witness, your awareness, consciousness and spiritual self remains infinitely intact no matter where your body rests or what is happening in the physical world around you.

Now consider this: What if everything in the physical world your mind imagines beyond closed eyes is not really what you understand or believe to be solid matter?

Instead, imagine every physical object beyond the darkness were simply variations of subatomic, quantum energy? Empty space and microcosms of carbon, hydrogen, nitrogen, phosphorus and oxygen atoms, each composed of protons, neutrons, electrons and yet smaller particles all moving in a constant high frequency rapid vibration fabricating a multitude of possible shapes, sizes and densities.

In other words, all physical matter was composed of the same energy and microcosmic materials in varying densities.

That is the truth.

Solid objects are not solid at all.

We saw earlier, that when the smallest rapid-fire, vibrating subatomic element that manifests physical matter is further broken down to their true rudimentary nature, they are

Pure *Energy*.

We know that all physical matter is a manifestation of energy from within and as a unique extension of

The Energy That Is Everything.

All physical matter reduced to its basic unit is an energetic component of the

One Divine Consciousness.

Understanding all physical matter to be a manifestation of the one great energy,

> Closing your eyes again, in dreams or meditation, you might easily be (or at least imagine you are) in another city or on a planet in a different galaxy beyond where you believe yourself to be in this moment.
> You could easily place yourself in another dimension of time and space.
> We do it all the time in dreams, meditation and accidentally within fractions of waking seconds throughout the day. Have you noticed?

Diving deeper into this concept, you could physically and energetically transport yourself to a friend's house across the country or around the world, even be sitting on a cloud as easily as in a chair.

Try this,

> Imagine beyond closed eyes, that you are a giant redwood tree. Look down to your massive trunk and huge limbs. See and feel your thick bark, deep roots and broad branches. Smell the forest, listen to the sounds.
>
> What thoughts and awareness might you have?
> What would you the *Witness*, your higher consciousness, have learned, enjoyed, been part of and present to over the previous 300 years?

Just close your eyes and take a few moments to warmly bathe yourself within

The Energy That Is Everything,

The Energy that is Divinely You.

Conflict and Confusion between the physical world and The Energy That Is Everything.

Our connection to multiple planes of reality can sometimes cause confusion and emotional conflict. Commonly flooded with overlapping information from our higher consciousness, thoughts in our minds and information from other planes of existence, all present as different voices in our head, equally substantial and simultaneously.

Which voice will we use in guiding decisions or expressing ourselves in the physical world?

An example might be the awkwardness felt in children of social ages who feel self-conscious, embarrassed or judged by peers and adults.

> Think about the child at social gatherings who is off alone, appearing to be talking with themselves and seeming fearful of other kids and social interaction.
> They may be considered unusual or an outcast by their inability for conforming to societal standards of behavior. Their imaginations and stories might be interpreted by family and friends as fantasy, science fiction and related to make-believe friends. These kids may be branded as autistic, with attention deficit hyperactivity disorder, depression, obsessive compulsive disorder or with other special needs labels.

Sometimes unnoticed or overlooked, these children are often highly intelligent, incredibly creative and abundantly productive with a little guidance.

What may appear in children as antisocial or unusual behavior might instead result from maintaining their natural, purer connection to divine consciousness.

With a less active filter for conforming to expected behavioral norms and invented social order labels,
These children allow themselves to interpret information from other dimensions while simultaneously living in the present.

Playing with seemingly imaginary friends in a futuristic interplanetary game, knightly jousting tournaments of the past or primitive play with dinosaurs, these children may be energetically in some other plane of existence living bits of those multiple realities simultaneously.

Since the beginnings of *civilized* man emerging into shared communities,
Avoiding rejection, banishment from a clan, suffering shame, embarrassment, fear or being killed, tribe members behaved within the confines of agreed social behavior.

Children naturally less inclined to conform within societal rules and social norms communicate their more authentic thoughts and behaviors.

Maintaining a purer connection to the energy of their origin, children will verbalize and express their true creative, stream of consciousness thoughts and feelings where most older children and adults are unwilling for fear of being judged or embarrassed.

When a child or adult is behaving in a manner appearing odd or antisocial to others, they may simply be expressing themselves from information being heard or sensed from an alternate reality by their connection to Divine consciousness.

They may experience an inner vision, seeing, feeling, hearing or knowing what is *not being said* in social interactions.

As an example, most people have learned and practice social graces even in the face of knowing someone is not saying what they really mean or may not be telling the truth. There are agreed-upon appropriate behaviors for gracefully accepting these mannerisms in social situations. Social etiquette for responding to someone lying could be a smile and nod or pretend that what they are saying is true.

Being more connected to our place of origin, we find greater difficulty in behaving with such social etiquette and instead, hear and express our authentic thoughts and feelings which may be in conflict with social reality. We are experiencing a greater understanding of deeper truths, including misrepresentations of reality.

Call it a knowing or intuition.

As a result of this connection to their authenticity, rather than act within social etiquette that is out of alignment with their truth and would be awkward or confrontational, these children might just run away, a behavior that would be considered socially odd. The person who was talking with them might be thinking, "Why didn't that child (person) interact with me while I was talking (even though I wasn't meaning what I was saying)?"

Conforming standards, social etiquette, tribal behaviors and expectations have created a societal oath for accepting what another person says even when we are in disagreement or know it to be untrue.

An assortment of human survival rationales exist for societal agreement that supersedes what we might sense or know to be reality.

Being connected to your authentic self, linked to The Energy That Is Everything and unified with your truth,

Lao-Tzu in the Tao te Ching, suggests,

> "Seeing without eyes, listening without ears and speaking without words."

While thoughts are believed to be completely private,

Through the interconnected fabric of Universal Consciousness, within the matrix of The Energy That Is Everything,

All thoughts are an open book to everyone from the past, present and future, beyond time and space.

We only have to accept the possibility, have awareness, be listening and willing to know.

The ability to know and understand what someone means beyond their words or actions is an infinite, natural gift, existent since the beginning of man, present in every life form and originating from that place where we all connect within

The Energy That Is Everything.

How did we communicate before there were words...?

Those children who might appear to behave oddly by socially accepted standards without concern of typical societally agreed behaviors, are likely receiving an overload of information from a multitude of dimensions and having difficulty keeping them all in order.

It is as if God's voice (Divine Source, The Energy That Is Everything) is giving them one set of guidance, they have their own thoughts and social norms or someone in their life is telling them to think and act differently. They are confused by simultaneous direction from higher sources, their own inner desire and those from the physical world.

They may hear one directive from family or friends while knowing another truth through intuition or a higher source.

This creates confusion in how they are *supposed to* behave. The child may shutdown to social norms, run away and hide, over-react or get angry as a protective mechanism for keeping others at bay while working towards reestablishing an inner truth that is comfortable and safe.

They need time to process and understand what is real for them.

Spontaneous Innovative Revelations!

Spontaneous, expansive, creative thoughts, discoveries and ideas that seem to just *pop into our head*, may not be our own at all. New ideas and concepts can be delivered or extracted from our higher level of consciousness voyaging within The Energy That Is Everything and Universal Consciousness. Other times, these thoughts and ideas might arise out of diverse resources and entities from different dimensions, past or future, without our conscious awareness.

In these moments we might think,

Where on earth did that thought or idea come from? or
I don't know how I thought of that!

In Jane Roberts *Seth Speaks*, Seth refers to this phenomenon as *bleed-through information*. Knowledge that bleeds through the boundaries between physical reality and a humanly indescribable flow of unified metaphysical energy where everything is connected.

A new idea flashes across our mind and we have multiple options for examining it. Some people might ignore the thought or simply find it curious. Others may embrace the concept, taking action, studying, developing and growing the idea into something special and unique.

Have you ever noticed the flow of creative thoughts and actions coming from the minds of children, where the information is clearly beyond what they could have possibly learned or known? These are ideas and concepts plucked from other dimensions often with limited ability to process or express the information.

A scientific, futuristic thought might have arisen from a place they are simultaneously connected-to in the future. Game playing from a historical era may be a reflection of who they are or were in a past or concurrent plane of reality.

A child deeply focused and operating in this manner might have trouble differentiating what is real in physical reality compared to what is being received from a parallel existence, thereby appearing socially unusual or atypical.

This can only transpire through a beautiful, fluid, open and loving connection to The Energy That Is Everything.

Historical figures in science, music, philosophy and art have fit nicely into the categories of the socially odd, unusual, slow, depressed, autistic, attention deficit or obsessive-compulsive disorders. This group could easily include Albert Einstein, Isaac Newton, Abraham Lincoln, Winston Churchill, Thomas Edison, Alexander Graham Bell, Nikola Tesla, Mozart, Leonardo DaVinci, Beethoven, William James and Temple Grandin to name just a few.

> What would have happened if these important historical icons had been placed on medication as children to cure what was considered a medical condition? Would their thoughts and ideas have been dulled or modified? Would they have taken the actions and followed through on their ideas? Unfortunately, this is happening far too often in our modern times.

These notables in some part, channeled their discoveries and ideas from dimensions beyond the physical that forever changed the world. Knowingly or not, they all accepted and acted upon ideas and knowledge received not only from their intellect and higher consciousness, but also information gleaned from other planes of existence.

They were spontaneously and creatively, operating from the place of their origin. Acting with authenticity from their connection to The Energy That Is Everything, from the one unified Divine consciousness.

Other planes of existence or realities so to speak, are simply components of and within The Energy That Is Everything.

Our Spiritual Self, the Soul, is also a unique extension of and from within this same energy.

Now he has departed from this strange world a little ahead of me. That means nothing. People like us, who believe in physics, know that the distinction between past, present and future is only a stubbornly persistent illusion.
A. Einstein.

The Soul

In a similar manner to a thermostat altering room temperature, our brain and mind with consciousness as the conduit, have the capacity for raising or lowering the degree of *awareness* and *connection* to our Spiritual self (the Soul).

By increasing or decreasing the depth and strength of one's connection to their Spiritual self, most easily accomplished through the practice of meditation and dreams, our well-being, physical and spiritual needs are met in the most efficient and understandable manner.

The eternal nature of our Spiritual and conscious-self existing well beyond the physical body and thriving in multiple planes of reality,

Remains constant after death.

Consciousness and Physical Dysfunction

Some disease and illness may alter our physical brain and thinking mind.

Examples might include, Autism, Alzheimer's Disease, coma, stroke, psychological and psychosocial disorders, lapses in memory and other mind-altering human conditions where communication is absent, skewed or limited,

> Giving an appearance of diminished or lack of consciousness.

In such medical conditions and not well understood nor easy for family and friends to truly grasp,
While the thinking mind has been modified or subdued,

> Consciousness is maintained, fully functioning and intact.

> The soul remains unchanged.

The Spiritual self and consciousness cannot be altered by physical condition.

> *We* are not prisoners of our body...

Medical conditions can diminish or alter our brain's awareness of consciousness disrupting the link between thoughts within the brain and communication to and from our conscious selves.

When the brain is altered physically or biochemically, it is unable to interpret, communicate or express our conscious or Spiritual self to the physical world.

It is not though, an alteration of one's consciousness or Spiritual self.

In conditions that appear to alter or suppress the mind, people maintain full consciousness, the ability to think, feel and comprehend.

What they lose, is their anatomical capability for physically or verbally expressing their thoughts or conscious intelligence.

Physically debilitating conditions redirect one's focus from the current plane of existence to other important work and activities in additional multi-planed, non-physical realities.

The Brain's ability to interpret higher consciousness and express that information through the physical body is interrupted.

Some reasons for reducing the connection and communication with the current physical environment might include completion of intended interests during this incarnation, more important work in another reality or one's current physical existence being too overwhelming.

As a form of self-preservation or transition,
This state may be temporary or permanent.

It's a personal choice.

There are times when a person may be finished with their earthly work though not ready to physically leave family and friends. These family and friends also may not yet be prepared to deal with their passing and keep an intention for their continued presence.

> An alteration of physical mechanisms interpreting and expressing one's consciousness to the world at large, may also be a choice.

Even in these states of being, thinking, consciousness and the Spiritual self remain fully intact. They are just not organized and expressed as we are used to seeing during this incarnation.

> There may be greater work to accomplish in different realities that would be far too frightening or overwhelming to simultaneously comprehend and explain to oneself and others during this an earthly incarnation.

Do these conditions make a person ill, abnormal, crazy, unconscious, dysfunctional or even unhappy?

Absolutely not.

In mental states that *seem* unconscious, people may appear irrational and unable to physically or verbally express themselves (actions and function) as expected compared to that person's typical, socially accepted behavior.

They are though fully aware, conscious, thinking and spiritually alive.

In fact, they are just as aware and conscious as you are reading this book.

Sometimes people simply need a break from a physical reality.

Some may return and some may have permanently moved-on, focusing greater awareness, consciousness and spirit elsewhere.

Consciousness is incalculably larger than the mind and brain.

Our Spiritual self is infinitely larger than consciousness.

> As a unique expression of our Godliness, the soul is a distinct and unique extension of The Energy That Is Everything.

The Soul is completely free and independent of all physical form.

> As eternal Spiritual Beings of energy, we are enmeshed within the divine fabric of, and extending from The Energy That Is Everything.

Chapter III

DEATH & SPIRITUALITY

What happens to "*Us*" when we die?

Nothing Happens

to "*Us*".

In the earthly event referred to as death,

Our physical body from this incarnation

Is simply recycled.

We are not our physical body.

Remember,

Without beginning or end,

We are Spiritual Beings having a physical incarnation.

What happens to our Spiritual Selves when we die?

Nothing.

Physical recycling is not a defining point for our Soul at the moment of death.

Our energetic Spiritual presence persists as boundless energy unconfined by the boundaries of a mortal, physical body during any particular incarnation.

Always has been and always will be.

An outer skin does not retain or harness the Energy of the Spiritual being we are.

Who *We* are dwells far beyond the limitations of our body.

Using words such as *Life* and *Death* in themselves establish earthly confines of time and space,

Limiting the human capacity to understand realities beyond the physical.

Death is no more than a time / space descriptive agreed upon by the masses, as a tool for describing what transpires when our physical body is recycled from this incarnation.

At the moment of Death,

Without a Blip,

Our Spiritual Beingness, our Soul

That unique, dynamic divine energy and blueprint
of who we are,

The *I AM*

Remains constant in the universe.

Without a missing a beat.

The relationship between our spiritual self and death might be compared to an actor at the end of a theatrical performance.

The actor performs the role of a character as if they are truly that person.

Simultaneously, she resides within another reality, the role of someone living an entire life outside the theater.
At times, her attention and focus are greater on who she is being in the play and other times within the same life experience her attention is focused on who she *really is*, outside the play.

While *being* in both roles fully, when the show ends (as completing a physical incarnation), the performer sheds her costume and character (as when the body is recycled).

Who she is outside the theater remains present and unchanged as always (like her Spiritual being of energy).

Shedding a physical body at death is not unlike removing the costumes and character in a play.

The nature of who we *really are*, are remains the same.

Without a blip.

In the moment of death,

Subject to the state in evolution of our relationship between the physical self, higher consciousness and Spiritual self,

Our body dropping away may go profoundly unnoticed.

In other words, physical death may be initially undetected by our thoughts and feelings persisting as if we had not died at all.

Because *we* haven't died.

There may or may not be a realization
your body has fallen away.

Taking a breath as usual, you might be unaware you did not take the next breath!

Or

Imagine walking down the street and not having noticed your body had dropped away a half a block behind you!

Your physical framework has run its intended course for this earthly adventure, passing from a simple three-dimensional existence quite naturally.

Consciously and Spiritually,

Who you are

Continues to thrive in a multitude of parallel realities and multidimensional universes simultaneously

As has always been the case.

Without noticing,

> Each night we transition from wakefulness into a mystical dream state or anytime we choose, shift our focus from physical reality to multidimensional, transcendental states of higher consciousness through meditation.

In the same manner,

> Whatever may be happening physically or how our body might be reacting at the moment of death,

There is no sensation, transformation or change,

> In *Who We Are*.

Only a massive

> Release of Love into the universe.

The physical passing of another human being can be a stressful and emotional experience for survivors.

It can also be a very loving and beautiful event.

Along with death comes the release of all physical world pain, worry and limitation,

Opening new and freer connections and communication with family and friends filled only with love and joy.

Being open and aware, you may be feeling a new, indescribable empowering closeness to your loved one you never before experienced.

It is from this most beautiful, loving and vibrantly powerful connection, people often think or say something like,

I feel like they're still here!

At the moment of death;

> We lose the physical limitations of the most recent incarnation.
>
> We become free of any discomfort associated with that embodiment,
>
> While maintaining the same awareness of our surroundings,
>
> We retain our consciousness, thoughts and
>
> Our Spiritual Selves remain unchanged.

As Beings of Spiritual Energy, unique extensions of and from within The Energy That Is Everything,

Our soul and higher conscious-self remain connected to everyone you ever touched emotionally or physically during each incarnation.

Only now that link is free of earthly complications and limitations.

We can more easily and freely connect with anyone from the past, present or future, void of life's disturbances, pain or limitations of time and space.

In Quantum Physics;

Laws of Thermodynamics Read:

"Energy is neither created nor destroyed but can only be converted from one form to another."

And

"In any process, the total energy remains at large in the universe."

We are eternally Beings of Spiritual *Energy.*

While having any adventure in physical form,

We are the same energetic, Spiritual entity, the soul, before, throughout and following that physical experience.

The Laws of Thermodynamics affirms the fact that nothing happens to the energy that is *Us* when our physical structure is recycled.

We are Spiritual beings acting uniquely within and extending from the fabric of The Energy That Is Everything.

That Eternal Energy is composed of the
Divine combination of

Every-Thing,

And is the Energy that manifests all physical matter.

Call it God by any name, as it is all Gods in the form of one
Loving, Knowing, Omnipresent Divine Force.

Our soul, the energy of who we really are,

Is a unique extension of this God Energy.

Microcosms of life and death occur constantly within our own body everyday throughout our lives and without any awareness.

> Every cell of the body blooms from undifferentiated origins, growing into specific full functioning units that are constantly recycling.

Without any awareness or concern, this life and death of cells is an ongoing and important process within our own body from birth to death.

> Our entire anatomy is regularly recycled.

We are completely different physical beings every few days.

Just as the cells of our body are constantly recycled, on a larger scale, our bodies grow into functioning units, have an earthly experience and are eventually recycled.

> Our Spiritual self focuses no more attention on this birth and recycling of our physical body than we focus on the daily cycle of birth and death taking place in the cellular structure of our own physical anatomy.

We take for granted that our body is functioning as it should without keeping track of the billions of processes taking place each day,

Just as our soul trusts the functioning and unfolding of entire physical incarnations from beginning to completion.

While dying might take us away from things we cling to,

Stuff,

Death does not take anything away From

Who We Are,

Nor does it alter the connections to people in our lives.

As a drop of rain diffuses back into the ocean,

Individual consciousness returns to the universal oneness.

Beyond the boundaries of time and space, this physical life and death process commonly referred to as, reincarnation, continues over and over in the same manner each cell of our body recycles

Having no bearing on *who we are.*

No matter how many incarnations we experience or in what physical form we choose, consciousness and our Spiritual Self remains intact.

Every-Thing in physical and metaphysical nature,

Is a manifestation of Energy.

Every-Thing is a unique extension of and from within

The Energy That Is Everything.

The Volume of Energy in the Universe is Always the Same.

Energy is Perpetual.

Energy is Constantly Changing Form.

Embrace the cyclic nature of all that is Physical,

And Love Eternal Nature of

The Energy That Is Everything.

In the grand perspective of the eternal universe there is no beginning and no end.

There is only the present moment,

Abundant with limitless adventure, opportunity, creativity, spontaneity, generosity, Love and Joy.

Time and Space

Human-made words and concepts, time and space were created for communication between humans.

A method for meeting a friend at Starbucks or to avoid burning the turkey.

Time and Space are simply agreed upon fairytales and fabrications.

In nature there is no time or space,

Everything is Infinite.

I might say, "I live ten miles away."
But there is no such thing in nature as ten miles away.
Ten miles is just a contrived interval within *infinity*.

Flowers and birds live full, beautiful lifetimes with no concept for time or space.

Animals migrate and hibernate without a clock, eat and sleep when they're supposed to, and live life fully without the knowledge of clocks or calendars.

The tide ebbs and flows, weather changes, the earth rotates, sun and moon rise and set all as they are supposed to without the boundaries of time or space.

Beyond time or space,

In any given moment, we can close our eyes, dream or meditate, then bring to mind and consciousness any specific event or situation from the past or future.

So easily, we can reproduce and re-experience *exactly*, any previous incident just as if we were there, in the here and now. We experience the same age, the precise time frame, the identical feelings and without relevance to current age, place or physical condition.

> Whether 10 years, 30 or 60 years ago, we are able to feel, smell, taste and touch any event or circumstance as if it were here in this present moment.

> We can re-experience a highlight in our lives, a particular event or specific instant, a special moments with a friend or family, as a child, teen or any age, just as if it were taking place this very instant.

A 100 years ago, 1000 years ago or even 1000 years into the future makes no difference.

Rendering time and space the illusion they are,

> We can reconnect with a loved one or tap into the future bringing back an advanced idea and knowledge that will forever change the world.

Absent of life and death,

    Beyond time or space lies the place where we truly reside,

      Our limitless Spiritual self within

        The Energy That Is Everything.

Time, Space and the Material World,

Are irrelevant in relationship to

Who We Are.

Before Birth,

Throughout Life,

And After Death,

The Energy of Who We Are

As Unique Expressions of

The Energy That Is Everything,

Remains the same.

But do not let your infinite nature as a spiritual being of energy

Take life for granted,

Each incarnation is an opportunity for

Living Your Greatest and Fearless Life Adventure.

Avoid being one who waits for impending death to be their teacher,

> Bringing them into the present moment with an urgency for living, as in,

> *You have one week to live, what will you do?*

Each day,

> You have a choice for stepping up and

>> *Living Courageously Now,*

>>> In each Present Moment.

If you knew you were not going to wake up tomorrow or in a week,

> What would you be doing now?

> How would your thinking and priorities change?

> How many weeks have you wasted already living in the past or future?

Pause reading here:

> Take 10 minutes or as long as you need and journal what you would do if you only had one week or one month left to live.

Live Courageously,

Live Boldly,

Live in the Present Moment,

Live as if this life were your Last,

Live every incarnation as if it were Your Last.

Dying or leaving your body is not a requirement,

For experiencing your eternal nature

And that ever present connection to God,

The Energy That Is Everything.

Having a divine adventure,

Expanding in higher levels consciousness, in spiritual development, creating meaning and purpose or realizing the oneness within The Energy That Is Everything are only some of the opportunities taking place throughout each incarnation.

A physical incarnation can be an instrument or step towards greater purpose, purity of spirit and godliness.

Living one's life is not simply a race in achieving a particular goal in any single earthly incarnation.

When we pass from this physical incarnation and forevermore,

Consciousness remains the channel for communication between our Spiritual self and universal consciousness, including a connection to the minds of those still living,

Our Spiritual self continues to communicate and interact with the souls of others living and passed, within The Energy That Is Everything, as always.

A conscious and spiritual relationship remains intact to those you interact with during each incarnation.

Even those who have reincarnated elsewhere, and in any form, through the multitude of parallel realities we maintain an eternal, dynamic energetic connection.

At any given moment in the earthly time and space,

> We can connect with a parent, child, family member, friend, teacher or anyone of interest, alive or passed.
>
> Manifesting this interaction is as simple as closing your eyes, getting quiet and calling upon them. You can see them, notice their aroma, touch them, have a conversation or ask a question.
>
> If you are willing and aware,
>
> You will be able to see and feel them standing before you as if always present.
>
> If you are listening,
>
> > They will always answer.

Death,

More accurately,

Freedom from a physical incarnation

Invariably a personal choice,

Transpires exactly when it is supposed to happen and not a moment sooner.

Prematurely, *intentionally ending one's life*,

Is never helpful and of course,

Results in consequences.

Ending one's physical incarnation intentionally as by suicide, requires a return to re-live every moment from the beginning of that previous life experience right up to the same point of interpersonal discord that lead to a suicide.

Then, to continue that life experience to its natural completion.

There are no shortcuts...

No matter how long it takes, no matter how many lifetimes, that specific path will be re-lived over and over again until we grow through the reason that lead to ending a life short.

In other words, the life monotonously, keeps repeating itself until we have worked out what brought us to that point.

There is an obligation to re-live that life experience from the beginning to the point of self-termination and until we gain the skills for moving beyond the issues that created such an action.

KARMA

It is never helpful to intentionally end one's life.

There are no short cuts to lessons in higher consciousness and spiritual growth.

There is no escaping a single life lesson.

Whether this lifetime or the next, each self-generated lesson will have to be experienced and learned.

The penalty for short cutting a life lesson, is failure of moving to the next expanded level of conscious awareness and spiritual freedom.

The world changes with every thought and every action.

Perpetually nurturing and expanding the relationship with a higher consciousness state and deeper connection to our Spiritual self,

Each incarnation is an exercise and adventure in resolving and releasing restrictive, unconscious behaviors, thoughts and ways of being,

Moving us towards higher stations

Of Eternal Spirituality.

Supported by each physical incarnation, with minimal attention by our Spiritual self, our physical nature strives for peak health and optimal function while maintaining the most perfect unity with

The Energy That Is Everything,

This allows expression of our authentic nature,

Generating Spiritual Fulfillment,

Pure and Infinite.

While our physical form is recycled from this three-dimensional world returning to the earth as a rain drop melds with the sea,

Eternally, so far by comprehension by physical science,

Our Spiritual self continues its magnificent journey of Love, Compassion and Light.

Choosing a new physical incarnation within this same world, spiritual and conscious growth continue from the end-point of the previous life adventure along with new knowledge gained and experienced in between.

Once freed from a physical incarnation the magnitude of opportunities is tremendous. Unimaginable options and adventures present themselves. The preference is ours.

Reincarnation is a choice,

One which may be immediate or not.

Time and space are irrelevant.

New expansive, loving, compassionate adventures and endeavors may remain in a metaphysical realm or might return immediately to another physical state.

It's always a choice.

Chapter IV

SPIRITUALITY, JOY & HEAVEN

Love, Peace, Harmony, and Joy

Are goals for most people.

Sounds like Heaven.

Heaven is not a remote place you find yourself after dying

If you were good in your most recent incarnation.

Nor is hell a place where you are sent *if you had been bad.*

Heaven is

Having Everything you need,

Living in all the Love you could ever imagine,

Grasping Joy beyond what could possibly be dreamed,

Existing in a state of everlasting Harmony,

Being at Peace with every part of one's life,

Perpetually having a sense of Meaning, Purpose, Fulfillment and Love,

Heaven is *Living* and knowing you are

One with The Energy That Is Everything.

Achieving Heaven,

Is Connecting with the Place of Our Origin.

Understanding the de-evolution into man's distraction from her connection to Universal Consciousness and a look into the origin of language might bring an enlightening perspective to the concept of *Heaven*.

Think about the same measure of consciousness and spirituality having always been present to the same degree,

Even in our primitive ancestors.

Without the neuro-anatomical development allowing communication with words, primitive man was unable to verbally express what they were thinking and feeling as we do now.

So how then did primitive man communicate?

Before there was language, man communicated without words.

What does that mean?

> Initially without a voice, early man could only have communicated by a combination of *telepathy* and *intuition*.

> Both in a sense, lost arts though being revived.

This would indicate that prior to thoughts being attached to words, language and objects,

> Man was acting more directly from guidance by higher consciousness and a direct connection to their Spiritual self.

Where else would early man's thoughts and actions have arisen from?

The word *telepathy* might generate images of parlor tricks.

Consider instead that telepathy for those truly practiced in the art, is merely a feature of intuition.

> *Intuition*, as it is now, was primitive man's guidance by their innate, spiritual connection to Universal Consciousness.
>
> Without modern-day distractions, early man was more highly attuned to their Source, directing them in feeling, knowing and understanding best choices and actions in any given situation.
>
> Whether making decisions about moving residence, finding optimal hunting and gathering grounds, behavior within the tribe, fighting, peace, loving or protecting family, their actions arose from a less distracted and more direct connection to The Energy That Is Everything.

Over time and likely the result of an urge for control and dominance by an aggressive overbearing tribe member, in addition to intuition and telepathy, gestures and noises were employed to communicate, forcing others to behave as he or she demanded.

> The success of noises and gestures controlling other primates would have led to more specific commanding sounds. Progressively, these noises varying in pitch and volume would have been repeated and evolved into what we now understand to be words and language.

> As noises, gestures, words and language multiplied, less reliance and attention were paid to intuition and telepathy. The ultimate result was diminishing actions and behavior from guidance by one's connection to their Spiritual self.

This illustrates language development as one path diverting man away from the connection to their Divinely guided self. A path leading away from taking action authentic and Divine guidance.

The good news is, that more of modern culture is returning to guidance, action and living from that more primitive state of a pure connection to The Energy That Is Everything.

From Birth's first moment, we naturally and spontaneously live in the Here and Now, in each present moment.

Every need is met.

> Our experience is a flow of Love, Peace, Harmony and Joy.

> As a newborn child we come into this world already in Heaven.

Living out of *The Moment,*

Or

Living out of Heaven

Is a learned behavior.

To illustrate this,

A newborn and infant experiences only Love, Harmony, Peace, Pleasure, Joy and Physical Sensation.

The sensation of physical pain is always associated with only a few environmental or physiological occurrences:
>Hunger, fatigue, gas pain, cold, heat, a loud sound and hurtful contact with the skin.

>Most often, each of these needs are quickly met.

Hunger is resolved simply by feeding. Fatigue becomes corrected with sleep. Environmental discomforts are relieved by removing the painful contact, removing the noise, comfort by a care giver or the passing of a normal physiological process.

Immediately upon removal of an uncomfortable sensation, the pain or discomfort is gone and forgotten.

>There is no dwelling on pain and no memories remain.

>No past or future exists for the infant or baby.

>Life is being lived in each moment.

In "Be Here Now," Ram Dass describes children as;

"Divine Avatars,

Holy beings who have come recently
from our true *home* to teach (us)."

Infants and babies do not focus on the past or future.

They Live in the Moment.

As infants in our new experience of the world around us,

We flow naturally in the heavenly spaces of

Love, Peace, Harmony and Joy.

Moving out of harmony as a newborn into discomfort of any kind,

We innately manifest a resolution

And return to the balance of Love Peace, Harmony, and Joy.

As infants,

    We harbor no fear, anxiety, resentment, doubt or anger,

    All of which are *learned* thoughts and feelings,

Reminding us as adults, that

    Emotions we carry are not dependent on circumstances,

    Those thoughts and feelings are choices.

Fear, anxiety, resentment, doubt and anger arise

From living out of the moment.

An infant never worries about the next meal, nor does the infant have concern about the last meal.

Born new to this world, we have no thought of what to do next, what others might think about us, how much sleep do I need, where to go, how to be, what's on television, what if I can't stand up, am I early or late, how many calories should I eat, where is my cell phone or what time and day it might be.

Being moved and acting moment by moment and experiencing free flowing, spontaneous thoughts purely from the connection to The Energy That Is Everything,

An infant simply

IS.

Without expectation, without a thought of the past or concern for the future and only living each moment,

> Infants enjoy the comfort of their clothing or freedom of their nakedness.

> They delight in the sound of a parent's voice and peacefulness in silence,

> Take pleasure in being fed, in a warm sunrise or in complete darkness, seeing brilliant colors, the movement of leaves, a bird's song or a dog's breath.

> An infant cherishes the experience of being held or wriggling in freedom and giggling.

> They enjoy the sound of music or smell of a pet and rolling on the floor.

> Faces make them cheery and food delights them.

> Infants love being held, love being cooed and enjoy the stillness of a quiet moment.

Infant's consciousness thoughts and actions flow without effort like a tranquil stream babbling through a peaceful forest,

With a pure and unique connection to and extension from within The Energy That Is Everything,

> An infant simply IS.

We enter this world living fully within each Heavenly moment.

Past and future do not exist.

There is no effort.

We Simply Are.

We enter this world still living in Heaven.

Naturally and without a thought, infants reach out to meet a *need* as it arises.

Newborns have no need to control desires or cravings, nor do they compile a schedule of daily activities, have obsessive thoughts, worry about the future or focus on accumulating material possessions.

Infants are not driven by *ego* attempting to impress anyone, control anything, be in competition, seek approval or avoid activities that might shame or embarrass.

Ego has yet to be fabricated.

Freshly birthed on earth without limitations or constriction in thoughts and feelings,

Endlessly unified within, and uniquely extending from the energy of their origin,

Newborn and Infants, simply Are.

From birth to death, an entire physical incarnation can unfold powerfully and effortlessly when living in the moment,

Through the conscious link
between the mind and our Divine Origin,

Guided purely by our authentic Spiritual Beingness,

And from our eternal, energetic connection within

The Energy That Is Everything.

Intangible, feelings such as, fear, anxiety, doubt, stress, anger, resentment, guilt, shame, low self-esteem, ego, competition, neediness and control,

Are *Learned Thoughts and Behaviors.*

Thoughts, Feelings and Emotions are not real *things*,

They cannot be seen nor touched and only contain the meaning we have attached to them in our minds.

We are unable to carry a box filled with painful thoughts and emotions to be treated by the doctor.

Every situation brings choices for what thoughts and emotions we will be feeling and for how long.

Positive or negative, happy or sad, angry or joyful, good or bad,

All just made-up,
limiting words we clutch to so tightly.

Make the choice for how you will feel and think.

There is always a choice.

Seething in negative feelings and toiling with emotional pain is to be stuck and obsessed on *past* events or *future* possibilities that may never happen.

Experiencing immobilizing feelings is,

>To be living outside the Here and Now.

Through maintaining a deep connection to *The Energy That Is Everything*, we live within the present moment opening doors to guidance by our authentic nature.

Being in the present moment and acting from our true nature is to experience unlimited gratitude.

>Gratitude is Infinite.

Learned emotions and behaviors such as, fear, anxiety, doubt, stress, anger, guilt, shame, low self-esteem, ego, competition, neediness and control,

Are not the true nature of our Spiritual Being.

As an example, think about a child opening their first wrapped present with no preconceived ideas, hopefulness or concern for what might be in the package.

They just want to *open the package*.

Living in the moment, the contents are unimportant. The child just wants to dive into the joy and activity of *opening* the package.

Figuring out how to open the present, colors of the wrapping, textures and sounds of ripping paper is where the focus and joy arise. Tape sticking to fingers, dogs jumping in an endless mess of wrappings and being tangled in it all!

It's about the joy, laughter and high energy surrounding them.

At this age, a child may become uninterested in the process before the gift is fully opened. They have no interest for what an adult may have put be in the box and simply enjoy every detail of the process.

That is living in the moment.

As an infant and child,

We instinctively live perfectly in every divine moment.

The Diminishing Spiritual Link
(Acclimating in the Material World)

Parents always want the best for their children.

A parent entering this world at their infancy is pre-encoded with thousands of years in genetic legacy, then overwhelmed with guidelines, rules, protocols, instructions and expectations for how to live. They are a product of their environment growing up with all its embedded decorum, quirks and experience of family, friends and other role models, forming unique interpretations of everything they see and hear, all the information, the images and life experiences.

Then, they are expected to raise the next generation with no definitive how-to guide.

However child rearing may appear from the outside or is perceived by the child, every parent naturally does the best they know how, with what they have and from where they are.

Raising children, loving them, giving and teaching to the best of their ability, parents, family and society instill customs, boundaries, rules, morals and ethics. While many of these guidelines and teachings are important for successful integration of the child into a societal structure, unintentional limiting ideas, behaviors and feelings are instilled or interpreted by the adolescent that can build barriers to maintaining that purer connection to The Energy That Is Everything and their authentic nature.

The result,
Is interference of the original, effortless connection to, and functioning from our Divine Source.

Learned behaviors, expectations, needs, desires, approval seeking, ego and cultivating unproductive emotions can build barriers to *seeing one's true life path* while at the same time, creating hurdles to remembering that ever present connection to The Energy that is Everything and their Spiritual self.

Progressively over time, the child and eventually as an adult unconsciously veer away from their inherent joy and self-fulfilled needs, once so naturally present.

In effect, child-rearing may unintentionally teach children to feel dependent on outside forces, opinions and stimulation for attention and approval, giving power to others or things outside of themselves to feel good or validated.

This seeking joy from outside of oneself happens when living in the past or future and disconnected from one's place of origin.

Looking deeply into the eyes of an infant you might sense a vibrant knowledge, enlightenment and understanding that feels far greater than their physical capability to communicate.

Infants exhibiting this feeling of *knowing* are commonly referenced as *Old Souls*.

While infants, they remain naturally living in the moment and more purely connected to their origin within The Eternal Energy That Is Everything.

They do know and understand.

As an infant matures into childhood and by adulthood, that gleam of knowingness deep in their eyes to often becomes dulled by layers of limiting thoughts and beliefs.

Reaching Heaven as an adult,

Requires a process of re-opening the door to our enlightened
newborn self,

Peeling back the dense layers of learned, limiting thinking and
beliefs that have dulled the ever-present connection to our divine
origin.

Returning to a state of deep knowing and understanding,

On a quantum level, restoring the metaphysical network
between every cell of our body, mind and consciousness, with

The Energy That Is Everything.

Toiling on the past or focusing on the future

Hampers creativity, expansion and growth,
Bringing discord, feelings of fear, doubt and worry,

Skewing alignment with one's true nature.

Being in Heaven

Requires living in the moment.

The Tao Te Ching
(aka: The Dao = "The Way")

This 2500-year-old book of Taoism comprising 81 verses, a guide of ancient wisdom for finding inner virtue and integrity through re-establishing balance and alignment within the nature of all things

Says,

"A journey of a thousand miles begins with one step."

In other words,
>   Be in the moment.

Avoid focusing on immobilizing fears, doubts, worries, perceived limitations or even the goal itself.

Instead, do something now. Take a step,

>   Stay in the Moment.

Take the next action.
Even the smallest step.
Do anything that is part of moving you in the direction of your goal or objective.

Reminder;

You will never have everything you want and desire in life!

Because,

Once a specific goal or desire is achieved,

You will almost immediately want something else.

Life feeds us an unending stream of desires and goals.

And that is okay.

Worthy goals and objectives throughout a lifetime

Are prolific, important, positive and expansive aspirations

Creating a Journey.

They drive creativity, progress and joy!

Mistakenly,

People believe that achieving an objective or the acquisition of some-thing, will bring everlasting happiness, life satisfaction and feelings of worthiness.

Life goals might include an education and career such as, becoming a teacher, a doctor, owning a business or simply having a job.
One might strive toward a specific objective like owning a car, a house or rare collectible.
Others may desire the perfect relationship or a holiday.

Life goals and objectives are endless,

Though not endpoints.

Achieving a goal will not bring lasting happiness,

As soon as an objective is successfully attained no matter how grand, rare or expensive,

It will quickly be replaced by another urgent desire.

There will never be a single life objective

That will bring, love, peace, harmony or joy

For much more than a moment

In the big picture of time and space.

But,

Goals and desires should not be diminished.

They are incredibly important in one's tangible life and personal development throughout a physical incarnation.

Here is the key to understanding Goals and Desires:

Having a strong Desire, creates objectives and goals,

Establishing a reason for having a life Adventure,

A reason for a Journey.

It is within the Journey that Joy is found.

A Journey of a life adventure manifests meaning, purpose, creativity, education, challenges, world-changing productivity and rich, meaningful, joyful life experiences.

In other words,

> Goals and desires are not meant to make us happy when they have been achieved
>
> And are instead, *reasons* for a *meaningful life adventure*.

Rather than focusing on a result in the future bearing the illusion of happiness,

Have a goal,

> But focus on the joy of today's step in the process, Enjoying the moment by moment, daily challenges and successes of the journey,

> **Happiness is in the journey,**

> **In each present moment of the journey!**

Living from your Heavenly place,

From the infinite perspective of your eternal nature as a
Spiritual being,

Less attached to the idea that you only live this
one incarnation from birth to death,

You realize that a physical incarnation is not something
you *get*,

It is not something that *happens to you*,

A human adventure is

An experience you choose and create.

Life happens regardless of your presence in this incarnation.

> Whether you are here or not.

> Regardless of how you behave, act or react in the world.

Choose who you are going to be!

Every day you have a choice for what is important, for what gives you meaning, purpose, how you will contribute and whether you will take each step of the adventure in joy or fear.

Time Is Not Running Out

Important life choices are best made when passionately generated through one's authentic nature and connection with Source, not because they seem quick or easy.

A castle, beautiful and strong is not built in a day.

Remember, *Time and Space are Illusions.*

It makes no difference what life goal you choose.

Whether to gain an education, buy that perfect house, be in a loving relationship or career advancement.

It *makes no difference how long it will take or how difficult* it could be in achieving your goal.

The joy and successful feeling of achievement will be the same if a life adventure requires one day, two years or ten years.

But we already know that lasting joy and life satisfaction are not found in reaching the objective.

Lasting, Sustainable Joy and Life Satisfaction is accomplished throughout a deep, rich Journey along the adventure towards your goal.

Independent of time and space,

Leaping beyond fear and doubt,

Make meaningful, passionate life choices,

For goals you really love,

And be in the joy of each step on the journey.

Joy is what we create in each magnificent moment of a passionate journey.

Once a goal is reached, we bask for a moment in the success,

And are immediately ready to create another purposeful mission or objective so our next passionate and joyful journey can be embarked upon.

Passionate, purpose driven life choices will create more consistent joy throughout a life adventure.

Be grateful, taking pleasure from each moment, each step of life endeavors, activities and actions moving you closer to each goal.

Avoid dwelling in thoughts of steps being *easy* or *hard* and rather allow them to simply be, as an intrinsic point in the process of moving toward an impassioned goal.

Love, peace, harmony and joy are always choices throughout every stage of an adventure.

A journey of a thousand miles not only begins with "the first step" as Lao Tzu points out in the Tao,

But continues by being present within every step thereafter.

Step after step, perpetually *choose* to live in the joy.

Happiness is all in the Journey.

Joy of the Journey is found in the present moment.

Happiness is living fully in the present moment.

Avoid dwelling on the last action or the next one. This is living out of the divine moment.

Living and creating a most productive and fulfilling life requires constantly releasing distracting thoughts that might hold us in our past or in the future.

Be in action mode! Take the next step immediately as opportunity arises without over analyzing what may or may not get in the way.

Then let go of expectation for any particular outcome.

If we take every action in each moment of a passionately guided path, we avoid distractions from our joy.

In the next moment where a new opportunity arises whether a minute or a week later, we again take action and let go of expectation.

Eventually there is no motivation needed to take the next action and no need to be thinking, toiling or living in the past or future.

Working in this manner becomes a divinely guided opportunity for yielding magnificent returns.

Taking each action that presents itself removes any thoughts from our distracting *consciousness plate*, clearing all past or future from our minds and leaving only the present joyful moment.

This Moment is Divine.

This Present Moment is Heavenly.

It can take practice to live in the moment.

Connecting to the Divine moment can be easily achieved by,

Forgiving:

Yourself and others for past situations you continue to hold onto.

While forgiving does not condone poor behavior and horrible events,
> It releases the negative energy you carry around anger or resentment contributing to illness and unhappiness.

You only harm yourself carrying anger and resentment.

We are always doing the best we can at the time for where we are in our evolution and ideally intend to behave from the highest and best place moving forward.

The past is the past and cannot be undone.

Release the distractions and limitations that thinking about past events hold over you.

Releasing anger and resentment is not a one-time deal.

Forgive at every opportunity and you will have the freedom of greater health and joy.

Let it go.

Connecting to the Divine moment can be easily achieved by,

<u>Being Grateful:</u>

Grateful for what you have in your life in this moment. There are probably hundreds or thousands of things you can be grateful for right now.

> Make a list of 10 things you are grateful for each morning and your day will begin brighter and more joyful.

Grateful for what you have enjoyed in the past,

> Anytime you are feeling low, stop, close your eyes and think of 5 things you are truly grateful for in your life.

And Grateful for what lies ahead,

> Think of one thing right now that you are grateful for in your future.

> And be grateful for all the unknowns, the surprises that lie ahead!

Connecting to the Divine moment can be easily achieved by,

<u>Release Focusing:</u>

On the Past or Future.

Rather take any action available in the moment.

"Always do everything you can"
Until there is nothing left to do and
Nothing to toil over in your mind,

Then release expectations for outcome.

Trust in Divine Order.

Meditate,

Be in the flow of this Divine Moment.

That's It!

Being in the joy of each Divine moment can be effortless.

With just a little practice,

Allowing the flow of inner authenticity and truth,

From your Spiritual self within the connection to

The Energy That Is Everything.

Achieving Heaven;

Is Living within each Divine Moment.

The grand show is eternal. It is always sunrise somewhere; the dew is never dried all at once; a shower is forever falling; vapor is ever rising. Eternal sunrise, eternal dawn and gloaming, on sea and continents and islands, each in its turn, as the round earth rolls.

John Muir

Chapter V

HEAVEN

Is Not A Destination.

You're already in

Heaven

You're already in Heaven

We are eternal, infinite and inexhaustible

Beings of Divine Energy.

You're already in Heaven

Who we Are,

Resides far beyond the bounds of physical form.

You're already in Heaven

Though our body may recycle over and again,

Our Spiritual Selves continue

Without a blip between physical incarnations.

Every life decision is best forged naturally,

Through the purest, most meaningful, heart centered intention,

Arising of Divine origin from your relationship as a

Unique extension of

The Energy That Is Everything.

You're already in Heaven

All you need to live

In Love, Peace, Harmony, Joy, Contentment and Happiness,

Is ever present in each Divine Moment,

Always.

You're already in Heaven

Living in the present moment,

In each Divinely Guided moment,

Is living naturally in Heaven.

You're Already In
HEAVEN

EPILOGUE

The most elegant interpretation of the Tao Te Ching, can be read in Dr. Wayne Dyer's "Change Your Thoughts, Change Your Life." In two of my favorite verses he suggests in the 8th verse "Living in the Flow" and the 43rd verse "Living Softly," to live as water. The Tao says, *the softest of all things override the hardest of all things.* Dr. Dyer notes that hardness is not strength. He describes patiently, quietly, effortlessly and gently, water will carve deeply even the hardest of marble and granite stone though the hardest of stone will not change water. All one has to do is look at places like the Grand Canyon in Arizona, Yosemite Valley of California and Colca Canyon in southern Peru or even a local stream and waterfall to see how water gently effects nature in very big ways and without even trying.

Water nourishes all things without trying. In Dr. Dyer's interpretation, he says, water *can't be held or squeezed but only experienced through relaxed hands, if allowed to flow will stay pure, never seeking a high spot above it all.*

While essential to maintain life on earth, water *tries* to do nothing. It is written in the Tao to *perform without action.* Water has no intention or plan to do any of the things it is used for in life. Water treats everyone equally and does all this by effortlessly being in the flow of nature. It simply is.

As is true for all matter and non-matter, water is a perpetual form of energy. As an eternal form of energy, water is easily understood as liquid, ice or steam, evaporating to form clouds then transforming once again into a liquid, raining back down on earth where it will freely flow in this continuous cycle. Dyer appears to interpret in the 8th verse of the Tao, that living as water refers to moving in harmony with the present moment.

311

Know the truth of just what to do and where to be in each moment. Treat everyone equally. Be timely in choosing the right moment for every appropriate action.

My perspective for living as water is to naturally flow from within your unique connection to The Energy That Is Everything (God as you know her). Living from our authentic nature comes in taking right actions without trying, knowing they arise from the place of our origin. In other words, move smoothly within the flow of nature without effort. Whether a surge of thoughts and ideas, physical movements or actions, let them be effortlessly guided by your true nature in the same way water creatively, joyfully and freely flows, being productive and nourishing to life and all without trying.

Living in this way, thoughts and actions pass effortlessly what may have previously felt like obstacles and barriers. When flowing from within one's connection to Divine Source, there is no resistance.

      AS WATER IS IN LIFE,

         DIVINE ENERGY AM I,

            POURED FORTH INTO NATURE.

Dr. Robin Lloyd Futoran
©2010 / ©2020 X ed.

About The Author

Dr. Futoran practiced healing arts in Studio City, California for more than 30 years. He has taught post-graduate courses internationally on numerous subjects in the field of healthcare. During his career, he served as a leader in his professional international organization, published papers, developed technical diagnostic procedures and has designed a practical healing technique. As a chiropractic orthopedist he utilized his skills in clinical and physical medicine as an avenue to serve his fellow man, promoting healing, healthful lifestyles, guiding and motivating his patients to live in their highest joy.

Dr. Futoran now leads longevity and healing retreats, practices functional medicine, health and prosperity coaching, continues to write books, lecture and act in the capacity of consultant for other healthcare practitioners.

Understanding our innate ability to manifest the life of our dreams through the connection and guidance by Divine Nature, his mission is to guide those with interest in finding and navigating their unique and meaningful life path to health and joy, to aid in allowing people to get in touch with the power of their true nature in order to achieve their highest goals and objectives while living in a state of love, peace, harmony and joy.

Website: www.robinlfutoran.com

Email: drrobinfutoran@gmail.com

www.ingramcontent.com/pod-product-compliance
Lightning Source LLC
Chambersburg PA
CBHW052030090426
42739CB00010B/1853